Words for New Weddings

DAVID GLUSKER

AND

THOM BLACKSTONE

atmosphere press

Library of Congress Control Number: 2021924071

Published by Atmosphere Press

Cover design by Beste Miray

atmospherepress.com

Introduction

One of the wonders of life is the constant change that we witness around us. Things are constantly evolving and usually enriching our society and our individual lives. Sometimes the change is difficult and slow. Other times it happens in what seems like a brief moment in history. Small changes can lead to great transformations in our culture. But change is the single constant of life.

When the first edition of the book (with a slightly different title), *Words For Your Wedding* (copyright 1983), was published, the world was very different than the world we know today. Very few unmarried couples lived together. Those that did were looked upon with scorn by much of society. Children born to unmarried couples were seen as "disadvantaged" or "unfortunate," and the term "born out of wedlock" was a negative statement about children and their parents. Interracial marriages were still few and far between, having been illegal in some states until 1967 (when *Loving vs. Virginia* secured that right). In addition, members of the gay, lesbian, bisexual, and transgender community often quietly celebrated marriage in a "shadow world" without the affirmation of their community or (sometimes) family members.

Furthermore, the world was a different place in other ways. Personal computers were a new thing. Safety features in cars were limited to seat belts and airbags. Electric and self-driving cars were thought to be an unrealistic dream, and cell phones first became available to the public in the mid-1980s.

But our world is different today. It is improving in many ways, including our recognition that all of us are God's children and deserve to be happy. And it will be different in other ways thirty-five years from now. Society is dynamic, constantly changing, and—hopefully—improving. This revision of the original *Words For Your Wedding* is a recognition and celebration of love in our world.

As we have worked together to update and improve a tool for creative and meaningful services of commitment and marriage, we have done so with hope for future relationships and families. "Love one another" is a key mantra behind our efforts. We hope that you find these words helpful, and we wish you happiness and excitement as you choose "words for *new* weddings!"

– David Glusker and Thom Blackstone

Preface

A Journey Continues...

It is very humbling that, by the purchase or use of this book, you have invited us to be a part of the journey of your life. Whether this is the first time that you have considered a wedding or service of commitment, or the second or third time that you are prepared to make a public pledge to a life partner, we are thrilled that you have chosen to let us have a small part in that moment by offering the suggestions and resources of this book.

More than thirty-five years ago, *Words For Your Wedding*, a workbook designed to help couples plan their wedding services, was created to enrich the experiences of couples by enabling them to actually choose the words to be used at their weddings. Over the years, countless couples and clergy have affirmed the helpfulness and value of the book. *Words For New Weddings* might be considered the "New Revised edition" of the original book.

We believe that the words you choose as you plan your

wedding or service of commitment are very important. Your wedding is not an insignificant event. It is more than a binding legal transaction. You could have chosen a simple legal marriage at a city or town hall, but you didn't. You have chosen to have a wedding, whether simple or complex. You want to pledge your love and faith to your partner. Therefore, the words you choose will reflect the depth of your relationship and commitment to each other. They are not just traditions or routines that you repeat, although that alone has value. They are expressions of affection and promises of love and loyalty that reflect your friendship, your love, and your desire to share your life journey with your partner.

Whether you have been planning your wedding for months or years, or perhaps have recently decided to take "the next step" in your relationship, this book is intended to be a helpful guide for you.

In our experience, as clergy having served various communities for more than forty years, and having officiated hundreds of weddings, most couples who decide to make the commitment to get married have given little, if any, attention to the words that will be used at their wedding. The words "I do" are the only part of the wedding service that most couples can recall. Furthermore, most couples believe that they would like the officiant to make all the decisions regarding the service or event. We believe that is a serious and significant lost opportunity.

If you were building a home, you would want to be able to decide how big it will be, how many rooms it will have, what materials will be used to build it, what color the walls will be, what kind of heat or air-conditioning will be included, and so on. While a generic house may be adequate, it may not be the best fit for you. It may not reflect your preferences or your feelings about the environment.

Your life journey and the building of your relationships is far more important than building a house. The wedding service is the moment when your share with your family, friends, and the community who you are as a couple and where you want to go together in life's journey. For the wedding to reflect these things, you need to invest some time and thought into preparing for the wedding. This book can be your primary tool in making your wedding an occasion that reflects your joy and love.

One other note: don't let the reception/party (with all of its details about cake, music, food, seating arrangements, decorations, and so forth) steal the significance of your wedding. Let the party be a celebration of the event in which you declare before God and the world that you choose each other. Make sure that you have a wedding that reflects who you are and what your relationship means as you enter the future.

We wish for you an event that captures the spirit of your love and the commitment each of you makes to the other as your journey takes you to new places and new heights in your relationships.

– The authors

Table of Contents

First Things First

How To Use This Book

We have designed and offer this book with the hope and prayer that it will be helpful to couples who are ready to take their relationship to the level of legal and/or spiritual union. We recognize that many couples are not familiar with or accustomed to planning worship events or other acts of legal or spiritual significance. We offer these words to help or enable you to plan your own wedding service or service of commitment, and to feel that the service is a reflection of what you want for your special event. For those who do not consider themselves "spiritual," we have also offered some "non-religious" options. Our goal is to help you create a meaningful wedding or service of commitment, which may or may not fall within traditional religious norms.

Our structural approach has been to begin each section or chapter with the words that are included in the "traditional" wedding service, which has been preserved in the *Book of Common Prayer* of the Anglican, or Episcopal, Church. Every chapter that offers choices regarding parts of the wedding begins by presenting the so-called "traditional" Christian offering. In addition, we also present a number of alternative choices, which have been created to offer the opportunity for you to "customize" your special event to the extent that it is a reflection of your feelings, beliefs, and preferences.

In our first wedding book, *Words For Your Wedding,* we included words from a number of other sources. The services of The United Methodist Church, The United Church of Christ, The American Lutheran Church, The Episcopal Church, and the United Church of Canada all contributed choices available to couples. Many faith communities have their own wedding services, which are found in books of worship of the denomination. If you are connected even remotely with a local church, temple, synagogue, or mosque, we encourage you to search out the standard or approved wedding service. You may not choose to use all of the words in the service, but there may be some words that speak to you and will enrich your wedding.

We do encourage you to read the traditional section in each chapter to give you a sense of what that section is about.

We have been very intentional about trying to present choices inclusive enough to be used at weddings that are bi-racial, multi-ethnic, same gender, or for other LGBTQ couples. This resource is intended to be helpful to all couples wishing to make their wedding a meaningful and personal time of commitment.

We suggest that you begin at the beginning. Decide what you want your wedding to be like. Do you want a "quickie" wedding, lasting about five minutes and just satisfying the legal requirements? Or do you want as much pomp and formality as can be squeezed into a service celebrating your love and commitment to one another? Most couples will choose something in-between. We encourage you to think about your guests at the wedding. Some have traveled significant distances to watch you make your commitment to one another. A five-minute service may not convey the importance of the commitment which you wish to share with your guests. At the same time, a three-hour wedding would test the loyalty of any friend or family member.

The "Order of Worship" section offers several possibilities for your consideration. The various offerings should not be considered as limiting your choices. You can design your own service, provided you have the support and approval of the person who will officiate the service. If you are involving a clergy person, or if the wedding is in a church or other sacred place, it is important that a degree of decorum is maintained and the sacred is acknowledged and celebrated.

Once you have decided approximately how long you want the wedding or service of commitment to last, and/or what the order of service or events will be, you can move to your specific choices. How would you like the officiant to greet the gathered assembly? Do you want music to be part of the event? What will the vows be like? Are you going to exchange rings? Do you want the officiant to offer any remarks or comments about marriage? These and many other questions can be answered as you make your way through the book.

The first edition (*Words For Your Wedding*) of our wedding book was available in two formats. One was a normal paperback book. The second was a pre-punched loose-leaf form, which could be used in a small "snap-ring" binder. Thus, the actual pages or choices chosen by couples could be put into the binder and used during the wedding service. That format is not practical in today's book market. Therefore, we actually suggest that, when you have made your choices for your wedding, you cut the pages out of the book, punch holes for loose-leaf binder use, and arrange them in the proper order so that the officiant can easily turn the pages and read them. This enables the wedding to go smoothly, without multiple sheets of paper being shuffled, and is quite easy for the leader. It also avoids copyright infringement issues.

You do not need to choose one of the choices from each chapter. You decide what you want to include. This book is intended to be helpful as you create your wedding. We want to say again: it is not mandatory for you to choose one of each category. As a matter of fact, we will get our greatest satisfaction from knowing that you chose the first part of one section, and the last part of another section. Or that you rewrote a paragraph to make it fit your desire or situation. We want to help and enable you to create your own wedding or service of commitment. Thus, we offer some "new words for your wedding."

FOR THE OFFICIANT

Whether you are a clergy-person, Justice of the Peace, notary, family member, or friend, if you have been asked to officiate a wedding (and have the authority of the State to do so), you will need some resources to make the event meaningful to the participants, including the guests. While one can always choose to "reinvent the wheel," we want to make things easier for you while also making the wedding or service of commitment as meaningful as possible for the couple to be married.

This book is designed to encourage the couple to choose the words that will be spoken at their wedding. In our experience—which covers many hundreds of weddings—most couples have no idea of what they want to happen at their wedding. They may know what band will play at the reception, who will provide food, what kind of decorations they would like, and much more. They may even know how they want to be dressed at the wedding. However, it is not unusual for very little attention to have been given to what will actually take place at the wedding. What will be said? What will the order of events (or order of worship) be? What vows will be shared? Will there be music? These and other questions can be answered using this book.

The couple gets to choose (or create) their vows, the opening words, any prayers, or any other parts of the service. They are presented with a wide range of options, which enables them to make simple choices and/or to combine parts of one option with parts of another. Most of the choices offered are new and have been written by the authors for this book. In every area, where there is a "traditional" offering, it has been presented at the beginning of the chapter. If a couple says that they would like a traditional wedding, we encourage you to say that you are happy to do whatever they would like you to do. However, simply ask them to go through the book and make "traditional" choices from each chapter. This exposes them to options which they may not have considered. In our experience, it is extremely rare for a couple to actually choose traditional words for every aspect of the wedding or service of commitment.

Once the choices have been made, you are then able to remove the appropriate pages from the book, punch holes in them, place them in the proper order, add any other notes or reminders, insert them in a "loose-leaf" binder, and have the service ready to go without loose pages, notes, or other material. This has proven to be very popular for clergy and others who have made use of the original *Words for Your Wedding*.

We hope that you find this book helpful and that you are able to offer a wonderful service to any and every couple who comes to you for your help in planning and officiating this important occasion.

AFTER THE CEREMONY

Following the completion of a wedding ceremony, the officiant—who serves as an agent of the State—is responsible to have the marriage license completed by getting the signatures of two witnesses, signing and dating it themselves, and returning it to the State. The couple may have particular people in mind whom they would like to serve as their witnesses. The traditional "best man/ woman" and the "maid/man of honor" have often been the "witnesses." There is no absolute requirement that these two people sign the documents. Any witness of the wedding may do so.

The officiant may wish to make a photocopy that can be given to the married couple, along with a "Certificate of Marriage," which can be purchased at many religious bookstores, online, or created on a computer. The certificate should also be signed and dated by the witnesses and officiant. Remember, it is the license that makes the wedding a reality. If the license is not completed and returned to the State, the couple is not married in the eyes of the State.

INCLUSIVE AND CREATIVE WEDDINGS

We do not pretend to represent the rich and deep cultural or historical gifts of a diverse humanity. However, it is our hope that our words might add something to wedding services from all cultures.

We believe this is as God intended, and the evolutionary journey of human development is continuing. Thus, we affirm and support the marriage of any two people who discover their ability to experience and offer love with or to another person.

All of the material found in this book can be used—or adapted, if desired—in services of commitment or weddings of two people from different racial or ethnic backgrounds, as well as in weddings of LGBTQ couples. If it seems that you can't find the words that you want for your wedding, we encourage you to modify or rewrite words so they are perfect for you. In some cases, it may make sense for couples to begin with a wedding service that comes from another religious tradition. A wedding or service of commitment is all about two people coming together to form a union that will last a lifetime.

While we want to be helpful, we cannot anticipate what will be most appropriate for every couple planning a wedding. Let's create your service together. Words from this book, including prayers, vows, etc., are offered in the hope that they will enrich the wedding. We are pleased to encourage options for those who are ready to take the step into marriage.

We hope that you find these "words for new weddings" helpful as you plan for your special day of commitment and celebration.

INVOLVING FAMILY, FRIENDS, AND OTHERS

There can be numerous places in a wedding or service of commitment where a guest or other participant can be invited to read, sing, or share. Scripture lessons or other readings, poetry, or lessons from appropriate sources can be read or recited by someone other than the officiant. Poems or the words of a hymn or song can enrich the event. Personal statements, possibly written by a family member or friend, can add a personal touch (not to be confused with toasts or words of congratulations shared at a celebratory reception).

The person officiating should have the authority to limit the readings or other material included in the wedding. This can be difficult if the officiant is a close friend or family member.

There are no rules regarding the involvement of family members and friends in acts of worship, commitment, marriage, and renewal. If having family members involved will enrich the moment, add joy to the experience, or strengthen family connections, feel free to do so. Children may create memories that will last a lifetime, provided they are old enough to follow instructions. Siblings, parents, grandparents, cousins, and friends can add to the meaning of this amazing moment of commitment and celebration.

On the other hand (there is always that "other hand"), we also recognize that not all families are as nurturing and "happy" as we might wish. Dysfunctional families are a reality of human history. You are under no obligation to include anyone who does not add to the joy of your wedding or service of commitment.

It is also true that it's not difficult to turn a sacred and special moment into what might be described as "a three-ring circus." As the old saying goes, "Too many cooks can spoil the broth." There needs to be a balance between inclusion and good judgment. An experienced officiant can guide you in determining what is appropriate and will enrich the wedding. He/she also needs to have the authority to say "no" when something inappropriate is suggested.

SPECIAL ADDITIONS AND SYMBOLS

Through the years, couples who have planned their own weddings, as well as those who have planned and officiated at weddings, have come up with some "special additions" to the services which have enriched the event for couples and their guests. Like the breaking of the glass in Jewish weddings, the symbol can become an important memory of the wedding event. We have included a couple of those additions for your consideration.

THE WEDDING CANDLE

After the guests have been seated and it is time for the wedding to begin, one of the ushers escorts the mother of one member of the couple (or some other family representative) to the front of the church, where she/he lights one of the two candles on the altar or table. After she/he is escorted to her/his seat, another usher escorts the mother of the other member of the couple (or some other family representative) to the front of the church, where she/he lights the second of the two candles on the altar or table. She/he is then escorted to her/his seat. Another option allows both family representatives to come forward at the same time to light the candles.

Following the exchange of vows and rings, the now-married couple approach the altar or table and each of them lights a taper from their "family candle." Then, at the same time, they combine their tapers to light a new candle on the altar or table. The symbolism of creating a new light, a new family, from two established families, can be a moving and significant moment in the wedding.

MIXING SAND

Following the exchange of vows and rings, the now-married couple each pick up a container that holds sand that has been colored and dried prior to the wedding. Together, they begin to pour the two containers of sand into a new container, swirling and mixing the sands into a unique pattern of their own creation. Upon completion, they seal the new container as a symbol of the creation of a new and unique family.

WEDDING BOUQUETS

Following the exchange of vows and rings, the now-married couple is approached by a representative from each of the two families of origin, carrying a bouquet of flowers. The flowers are given to each of the two members of the newly-married couple, who place them in a vase (possibly on the altar, or a table) one by one. The flowers form a new bouquet which can be the "family bouquet" for the new family.

OTHER OPTIONS

We encourage you to think creatively of other symbolic acts which may demonstrate to the community that you are now a legally and spiritually united family. Of course, all options should be approved by the officiant.

LGBTQ WEDDINGS

God has created us in wondrous and beautiful ways. Thank God that we are not all the same. While for many years in many cultures, men and women may have been forbidden from marrying people of the same gender, humanity is moving on, supporting and affirming love wherever it takes place. The decision of two men or two women to commit themselves to one another, and to share their journeys while affirming their love for one another, is equally worthy of celebration as any other marriage.

No less is true of God's transgender children who may have sought to correct a biological or physiological situation when their bodies have not been consistent with their minds and "hearts." Folks who have found it necessary to embrace their correct gender, or to live with inconsistencies of physical and emotional dimensions, should have no limits on the right to love and share life's journey with another of God's children.

We affirm the right of every human being to share and

receive love from other human beings. The basic desire and need to love and to be loved is not altered by physical, psychological, or spiritual differences. We are all children of God and deserve the happiness which can be found in a deep and profound relationship with another of God's children.

MUSIC

Love is a broad and widespread subject. Tens of thousands of songs have been written about seeing your love for the first time across a crowded room, first meeting each other, being captivated by a smile, your first kiss, or other moments in your journey. Most of these songs do not capture the depth of the commitment which is being celebrated at your wedding.

While there are a few popular songs that might be considered appropriate for weddings, most contemporary songs are not really about the commitment being celebrated on your wedding day. Good music is always entertaining, but we suspect that it is unlikely that you want your wedding guests to leave the wedding celebrating a concert, rather than focused on the giant step that you have taken by joining together in your marriage. Most couples do not want their guests to be distracted from the importance of their commitment to one another. On the contrary, they are sharing a sacred moment with the people that they care about most.

On the other hand, it should be said that there are some songs which have been written about the love which we are able to experience and the way we are able to share that love with our special partner. If your music is chosen carefully, in consultation with your officiant, it can enrich the wedding event in a number of ways.

Services of Commitment

Increasing numbers of couples are choosing to live together without getting married. Some of these folks have serious reasons to avoid getting married. Some have had one or more bad experiences with marriage. Some are afraid of the legal ramifications connected with marriage. Some do not want to formalize a "free spirit" relationship.

No matter the reasons, marriage does not seem like the best step for some couples. With that in mind, we suggest that a "Service of Commitment" (with no legal implications), may be an appropriate alternative.

We have included a chapter that offers two possible "services of commitment," but encourage you to think outside the box by using other options that fit your situation.

We suggest that you consider reviewing and using the various parts of this book, with the possibility of changing a word or two if necessary, omitting the words "Marriage" and "Wedding." As long as no "certificate of marriage," or "marriage license" is signed, it is not a legal wedding. You can put together a service of commitment or a celebration of your relationship with no legal implications.

For example, you can have a service, possibly involving a clergy (although any friend or family member can lead such a service), which calls a gathered group of family and friends together, has an opening prayer, asks if the couple wants to make a commitment to one another, offers an opportunity to say words of commitment, includes music, and even includes the exchange of rings, but is not a legal wedding. Of course, other items can be included in such a "Service of Commitment," but this gives you the idea. You can commit to one another without getting legally married. At the same time, couples who are not legally married forgo the protection which society makes for these relationships. These are very important decisions, legally and otherwise.

It seems appropriate to add a brief caveat regarding the possibility that in some situations, where marriage would change financial situations, due to social security payments to one or both parties being stopped, there may be a legal question which we are not prepared or qualified to answer. However, consultation with one attorney advised us that if no license is involved, no wedding has taken place. It may look like a wedding, feel like a wedding, and sound like a wedding, but without taking the needed steps to satisfy the laws of State and Government, including a license, it is not a wedding.

Non-Religious Weddings

While both of the authors of this book are United Methodist clergy, we recognize that many of the people who buy or use this book may not have connections with any organized religion. Furthermore, many of our readers may not believe in God, or any supreme being. References to a supreme being may actually be a distraction to some couples who want to formalize their relationship through marriage.

With that in mind, we have offered several "non-religious" options in various chapters, including the

"Order of Worship" section. You may prefer to call this "Program," or "Order of Events." The point is, you can have a wedding with no specific references to God or a divine presence. A civil or legal wedding does not have to include any references to God or religion. Marriages are actually civil events, creating a legal relationship between two people. They do not need to be religious in structure or form. Once again, we offer the possibility of choosing non-religious options when available, and/or creating your own options. It is not difficult to change a word here or there to make a paragraph or statement consistent with your belief or preferences. Be creative! Make your wedding uniquely yours!

We hope that you will find that this book encourages you to give some serious thought to how you would like to welcome your guests, what words you would like to share with your partner, and anything else that you would like to include in your wedding. We simply want to assist you in your commitment and celebration of your relationship.

PASSING THE PEACE

It has become popular in many churches to have a moment when guests (worshippers) are invited to turn to a neighbor, friend, or even a stranger sitting nearby to extend to them the peace of God. This not only helps people to get to know their neighbors, but it also reminds folks that we are the instruments of God, passing peace, kindness, and love through our words and deeds.

This act can be inserted into any wedding or other gathering in which faith in God is assumed by most of the participants. The worship leader or officiant may turn to the congregation and say the following: "At this time in our gathering, I invite you to turn to the people next to you, and the people in front of you and behind you, and say, 'The peace of God be with you (or other words of Grace and Peace).' The appropriate response is: 'And, also with you!'"

It is conceivable that in a "non-religious" wedding, or at any gathering, people might be invited to turn to their neighbor and say: "Hi, I'm David Glusker, from Maine." To which the person might respond, "Hi, I'm Thom Blackstone, and I'm also from Maine." This might be seen as an "ice-breaker" and could encourage the development of relationships and friendships.

RENEWAL OF VOWS

We are pleased to include a chapter for the renewal of wedding vows. This followed the suggestion of several friends who wanted a service of renewal that went beyond repeating the same words spoken years before. While for some couples the old words may hold the greatest meaning, others prefer a chance to express where they are today in their relationship.

Wedding anniversaries have always been considered special days by couples who have shared the marriage commitment. Woe to the husband or wife who forgets the anniversary of the day that he/she was united in marriage; the day that vows and rings were exchanged; the day that testified to the family and the world that they are now officially and legally a family.

Special gifts have been exchanged on anniversary days. A romantic card, a single flower, a meal at which you relive your courtship and wedding, or any one of hundreds of other possibilities can mark the day when you celebrate the anniversary of your wedding.

However, the greatest celebration of an anniversary remains "the renewal of your wedding vows." In today's world, husbands, wives, partners, spouses, significant others, and even family friends can suggest a service of renewal of wedding vows as a special anniversary celebration.

Special anniversaries, such as twenty years, twenty-five years, thirty years, and so on often become an occasion when vows are renewed, but any time is a good time to remember the words that witnessed to the world that you chose each other. There is no "bad" time to renew your commitment to one another. It is a way of saying, "Yes, I would gladly do it over again. I choose you as my life partner." With that in mind, we suggest that you consider using any of the material in this book to create a service of renewal of vows.

By simply adding or deleting words here and there, you can easily use almost any part of the words found in the section on "wedding vows" to restate your affection and commitment to one another.

In an effort to make it easier for you, we offer the renewal of vows chapter for your consideration. Do not feel limited to choosing only one of the possibilities. As is true with the section on wedding vows, there is no reason why one person can't use one vow, and the other person use a different vow. The vows should reflect what you feel and what you want to express.

The renewal service will have more meaning if the officiant does not ask the members of the couple renewing their vows to "repeat after me." We encourage you to copy your "wedding vows" or "renewal vows" on a card or paper, so that you can read them to your spouse. Or, better yet, memorize them, so that you can look at your partner as you speak them.

The Wedding

Accepting an invitation to attend a wedding is a little like opening an unmarked package: you may have no idea what will be contained in the package, just as you may have no idea what will be happening at the wedding. The wedding may take place at the beach, at a ski lodge, in a recreational hall, or at a church. It may last five minutes, or it may last an hour and a half. It may involve guitars and folk music, or it may include the sounds of a majestic organ in a great cathedral.

The decisions of choosing a location and creating an "order of service" are key to determining what kind of wedding you will have. The "order of service" creates an atmosphere just as the location does. Formality, or informality, is not determined by location alone, although one certainly influences the other.

What do you want your wedding to be like? How do you want your guests to feel during and after the wedding? What do you want your family and friends to "take away" from the wedding? Do you want solemnity and seriousness to prevail? Is a more celebratory atmosphere your goal as you exchange your vows?

It doesn't have to be all or nothing. While you may prefer formal over spontaneous, or vice versa, there may also be a "middle of the road" that will be just perfect for you. Now you get to decide: "What will my wedding be like?" Choosing the "Order of Service" (or order of events) will have a lot to do with the "tone" of the wedding.

As you look at the choices offered, remember that all of them are suggestions. You can mix and match to create just the order that you want. Such matters as the inclusion of music, adding readings from the Bible or other sources, having bridesmaids and ushers, and choosing your vows will determine what your wedding will be like. Of course, you may decide to change or amend your order of events as you review the various chapters of this book. We encourage you to spend a few extra minutes making the choices regarding your order of service. Your guests will appreciate it, and when you reflect on your wedding in twenty, thirty, or even fifty years, you will be glad you made good choices.

Traditional

(approximately 20-25 minutes)

Processional

Opening Statement

Charge to the Couple

Questions of Willingness

Presentation of the Bride

Exchange of Vows

Blessing and Presentation of Rings

Declaration of Marriage

Wedding Prayer

The Lord's Prayer

Benediction

Recessional

(Suitable music may be inserted at appropriate places)

Brief Marriage Ceremony

(Approximately 5-10 minutes)

Gathering (at front of church or other site of the wedding)

Words of Greeting and Welcome

Questions of Willingness

Exchange of Vows

Sharing Symbols of Marriage (rings, etc.)

Announcement of Marriage

Blessing and Sharing a Kiss

(Suitable music may be inserted at appropriate places)

For Blended Families

Processional of the Couple and their Children

Opening Statement

Charge to the Couple and their new step-children

Scripture lesson and/or other Readings

Exchange of Vows (between the couple, and to the children)

Presenting of Rings and other gifts (including the children)

Declaration of Marriage

Prayers

Benediction

Recessional

Contemporary Alternative

(Approximately 30-40 minutes)

Organ Prelude
Lighting of Family Candles on the altar
Processional
Welcoming words
Presentation of both participants by family members,
    or Best Man and Best Woman
Questions of Willingness
Musical Selection
Scripture Lesson(s)
Words of reflection (sermon)
Prayer for God's Love in this marriage
The Lord's Prayer
Exchange of Vows
Exchange of Rings
Musical Selection
Declaration of Marriage
Sharing a Wedding Kiss
Blessing
Recessional
Organ Postlude

For Senior Couples

Processional of the Couple and their Children

Lighting of Memorial Candles to honor previous spouse (or spouses) who have died

Opening Statement

Charge to the Couple

Scripture lesson and/or other Readings

Exchange of Vows

Statement of Support and Blessing from Family Members

Presenting of Rings

Declaration of Marriage

Prayers

Benediction

Recessional

Non-Religious Brief Wedding

(Approximately 5 minutes)

Arrival of Couple, Witnesses, and Guests
Questions of Willingness
Exchange of Vows (if desired)
Declaration of Marriage
Signing of Documents
Dismissal

Informal

Gathering in a Circle in a simple or natural setting
Welcoming Words
Scriptures and Poems
Friends and Family share words of support
Declaration of Consent
Vows
Sharing of Rings or other Symbols of Love
Act of Unity (lighting of a candle, pouring of water or sand into a common container, or other sign)
Prayers
Benediction
Greeting the Couple

Non-Religious Wedding
(Approximately 20-25 minutes)
>
> *Processional*
> *Greeting/Welcoming Words*
> *Presentations of Couple by Family Members or Friends*
> *Questions of Willingness*
> *Music*
> *Words of Reflection*
> *Exchange of Vows*
> *Presentation of Ring(s)*
> *Music*
> *Declaration/Pronouncement of Marriage*
> *Sharing a Wedding Kiss*
> *Dismissal*
> *Recessional*

Informal

Gathering (in silence)

A Candle is Lighted

*In the silence, several poems or statements about
marriage are read, with time for reflection*

Vows & Rings (done simply and with few words)

*The couple's hands are tied with a cord and the guests
come in silence and rest their hands on the hands
of the couple.*

Blessing

Silence

Benediction

Gathering Words

When someone visits our home, there are words spoken that transition our guests from the journey to the destination ("How was the trip? Did you find us okay? My, how tall the kids are!"). Part of the gift of hospitality is to communicate "welcome." We do so by drawing a sacred and loving circle around the fact that folks have arrived, we are here together, and our gathering has a purpose. It is no different with a wedding. The gathering words name the sacred circle into being. There are also practical words spoken here that help communicate the "norms" of our time together (expectations about photography or standing and sitting). It is appropriate to take note of the physical location (indoors or outdoors, a home of many generations, a garden sacred to a grandmother, etc.).

Traditional

"Dearly beloved, we are gathered together here in the sight of God, and the presence of these witnesses, to join together this man and this woman in holy matrimony; which is an honorable estate, instituted of God, and signifying unto us the mystical union which exists between Christ and his Church; which holy estate Christ adorned and beautified with his presence in Cana of Galilee. It is therefore not to be entered into inadvisedly, but reverently, discreetly, and in the fear of God. Into this holy estate these two persons come now to be joined. If anyone can show just cause why they may not lawfully be joined together, let them now speak, or else hereafter forever hold their peace."

(This may precede any of the following statements) Good Afternoon! It is my privilege to welcome you and to officiate at this wonderful event. (NAME) and (NAME) have spent considerable time and thought preparing this service. They want you to share one of the most important moments in their lives. With that in mind they, and I, invite those of you who want to take pictures of the wedding party and the couple, to bring your cameras and cell phones, and come up here and take your pictures. After this photo opportunity you are asked to put your cameras away, turn off your phones, and concentrate on the worship service which will unite (NAME) and (NAME) in holy matrimony. So this is a serious, one-time-only offer. Come on down, and get a few good pictures to help you preserve your memories of this wedding, then put your cameras away.

(If the above paragraph is used, sentences asking people to turn off their cell phones do not need to be repeated in the following statements.)

1. (Non-Religious)

Friends, Family, Neighbors, and other guests, it is my privilege to welcome you on behalf of (NAME) and (NAME), and to encourage you to (turn off your cell phones and) put other distractions out of your mind, as we witness an important moment in the lives of these two amazing people. This is a time of covenant and reflects the life-changing decisions which are being affirmed by this service. Each of you has a part in the lives of this couple. Together, we can add strength and love to their marriage.

2.

Brothers and Sisters, from (state/province/nation/tribe/ land) and (state/province/nation/tribe/land), the Holy God of all people and lands has brought together these two souls, (NAME) and (NAME). Today they begin to grow together in new soil, the soil of marriage: their roots to become one, their branches to entangle and sway together, their stories to be united. May their ancestors watch over them with approval, may their friends dance with joy at their union, and may the songs they sing be tunes of harmony and peace. Let us all come and worship as these two join their hands, histories, and journeys!

3.

I greet you in the holy name of God and welcome you to a special worship service during which (NAME) and (NAME) will pledge their love and commitment to one another. The vows, the prayers, the readings, have all been chosen by them. This is their wedding, and we have all been invited to witness it. (Please put your cameras and phones away, and) Let us worship God.

4.

Children of God, of all the places on the planet, we have chosen this place and this time to be blessed for the ceremony we celebrate today. (NAME) and (NAME) have invited us to this celebration, but we gather in the name of the God of all places and times who claims these as holy ground and sacred hour. Let the circle of this celebration be drawn wide, surrounding this couple with the love and support of all who wish them well. Let us bless and weave these lives together in the name of the one who created and called them to be one.

5.

This is a day which the Lord has made. Let us rejoice and be glad in it! I call you together as the people of God, as we gather to join (NAME) and (NAME) together in holy matrimony. This is a holy joining of two of God's children in a relationship that will last into the unknown future. In an effort to honor and respect this holy moment, (please put your cell phones and cameras away and) please focus on the words about to be shared in the presence of God.

6. (Non-Religious)

Fellow travelers on the journey,
Today we stand with (NAME) and (NAME).
From cities and towns,
We have come.
From far and near,
We have gathered.
From the days of your birth, adolescence, and adulthood,
We have assembled.
Now we bear witness to your vows, your love, and your joining together.
We hold you both in our hearts; you are not alone.
Let us come together to witness an act of love.

7.

I call you together as a congregation of God's people to witness the joining together of (NAME) and (NAME) as they exchange words of love and commitment with one another. It is a holy moment, so please (put your cell phones and cameras away and) focus on the act of love that you are about to witness.

8.

Holy and beloved, time is an ever-flowing stream, but today we make it stop for just a moment, this moment that we share together. In this moment, all time and all people are eternally present, all generations gathered as one. We name those who have gone before us in death, but whose love is represented here today: [*names may be read, candles lighted*]. May family and friends, present and absent, flesh and spirit, unite their voices of blessing over (NAME) and (NAME) who come to pledge their love to one another this Holy Day. Let us worship God together.

9.

I don't know what heaven is like, but I can imagine that there is celebration in heaven when two people exchange words of love and commitment with one another. We are gathered together to witness such a moment. (NAME) and (NAME) have come to this moment and this place to do such a thing. (Please put your phones and cameras away and focus on the miracle of love which you are about to witness.) Together, let us worship God.

10.

Fellow children of God: sunlight meets soil, and plants spring forth. Stream meets brook, and great rivers start to flow. Tune meets words, and beautiful songs are sung. Soul meets soul, and a new journey begins. Today we stand on holy ground, where two beautiful lives come together. They arrive at this sacred circle as two individuals, but they leave it as one family under God's watchful eye. Let us witness their joining, bless their journey, pledge our assistance to their marriage, and remind them that we walk with them in days to come. Come, let us worship together.

Opening Prayers

An opening prayer lets your guests know that you believe that someone greater than you is involved in your life journey. It is an invitation to the supreme being to be present and to bless what is about to happen. It is likely that such a prayer will add meaning for some, if not most of your guests. This prayer sets a tone or mood for the wedding as a serious occasion of commitment between two people.

It should be noted that the so-called "traditional" service does not include an opening prayer. However, many contemporary wedding services do. Adding a prayer, asking for God's blessing—not only on the wedding, but on the couple exchanging their vows of commitment—invokes a higher level upon the event. Prayer can "set a tone" for the wedding. More than that, it can be a moment of importance for the couple as they recognize the oversight of "the Holy One" on this important moment in their shared journey.

1.

Let us pray: God of Love, Grace, and Goodness, we call upon You as we gather in this sacred place to perform this wedding service. We ask you to make yourself known in this time of commitment, and these moments when we celebrate love among us. May the love which you have demonstrated throughout all human history be evident among us today. Help (NAMES) to love, honor, and cherish each other and to demonstrate their love by word and deed as long as they both shall live. Amen.

2.

Let us pray: Gracious God, you have called us together under the canopy of your love, summoning us to stand with (NAMES) on this unforgettable day. May we hear your voice in their voices. May we sense your touch in their touch as they reach out to one another. May we know your blessing as they are blessed. And may our hopes arise with theirs as they commit themselves to one another in this sacred place. Amen.

3.

Let us pray: Give us open hearts and minds as we gather to celebrate love within the human family, Lord. May the love symbolized by this gathering and the vows which will be shared be evident in all of us by the way we speak and act with one another. We pray especially for (NAMES) as they give and receive their words of love. May the spirit of this wedding abide with them and us for the rest of our lives. We ask these things in the name of Jesus, who personified love. Amen.

4.

Let us pray: Almighty and Triune God, at the heart of your being is relationship: Parent, Child, and Spirit, bound together in the dance of creation, redemption, and sustaining Love. As their friends and family, we hold (NAMES) in your light this day, confident that they will flourish under your watchful and loving eye. Bless their union and the love that they bring for one another. Amen.

5.

Let us pray: May the presence of Your Holy Spirit be evident among us today, Lord. May the beauty of creation be seen in your children as we gather here to worship you and to celebrate Love. And may our love for one another be reflected in our words and deeds today, and among all of your people. Amen.

6.

Let us pray: Holy God, creator of the earth and all that lives within and upon it, we know that you are always with your children, so we confidently call to you as we celebrate human love grounded in holy commitment this day. (NAMES) have walked with one another for a time, but today they set their eyes on a distant horizon. They cannot know what might be in their path, but they choose to travel it together. Surround this gathering, then, with your love and encouragement as we witness and support them in this sacred time. Amen.

7.

Let us pray: Help us to see You and Your love in this service which joins (NAME) together, Lord. May their words of commitment and faithfulness be a reflection of our desire to be faithful to you. Grant us an awareness of the presence of your Holy Spirit as we share acts of love and faithfulness. May this be a time when each of us renews our vows to one another and to You. Amen.

8.

Let us pray: Holy and gracious One. Throughout time, the power of love and attraction has enriched human lives and community. Today we stand with our friends as they stand with one another. We ask that your talented fingers and keen eyes weave these lives together as one. May they be for one another a bulwark against trouble, a protector of one another's gifts, and healers of one another's souls. Bless them, for they are wonderfully made in your image. Amen.

9.

Your love is beyond our understanding. Your gifts are greater than anything we can imagine. Your dreams and hopes for us are exciting and filled with promise. Help us to live within the boundaries of your love, your gifts, and your dreams for us. May this service, which celebrates love, fill all of us with hope for the future. Amen.

10.

Let us pray:
God of beauty, God of love: Come
God of the discouraged, God of the heartbroken: Come
God of the fearful, God of the lonely: Come
God of the joyful, God of the blessed: Come

CHARGE TO THE COUPLE

The two persons who are joining in marriage have brought themselves to an officiant or tradition that has expectations of the couple as they take their vows and continue their lives together. The "charge to the couple" expresses what those expectations are and encourages them to do their best as they dig deep within themselves to find the courage to make (and keep) their public declaration of love and commitment. The charge reminds the partners who come to embrace marriage of the seriousness and sacredness of what's about to happen.

Traditional

I require and charge you both, as you stand in the presence of God, before whom the secrets of all hearts are disclosed, that, having duly considered the holy covenant you are about to make, you do now declare before this company, your pledge of faith, each to the other. Be well assured that if these solemn vows are kept inviolate, as God's word demands, and if steadfastly you endeavor to do the will of your heavenly Father, God will bless your marriage, will grant you fulfillment in it, and will establish your home in peace.

It is at this point that some weddings include the question: "Is there anyone who can show just cause why this marriage should not take place?" This statement does not need to be included, but may be asked if the wedding couple wishes.

1.

(NAMES), as we stand before this gathering of family and friends, I call upon you to consider seriously the promises you are about to make. We have talked about these promises. You have shared the story of your friendship and love for one another. Now you are called upon to declare before God, these witnesses, and all the world that you are ready to move your relationship to the next level. Is it your desire that we continue with this wedding?

Couple answers together: Yes!

2.

(NAMES), today you begin a journey that will bind you together forever. "Forever" is a word that is seldom used in our world. Our likes and preferences can change at a moment's notice. "Forever," however, requires commitment, compromise, devotion, and deep love. Are you ready to make such a commitment to one another in the presence of God, family, and friends?

Couple answers together: We are!

3.

This is a day which the Lord has made. Let us rejoice and be glad in it.

We are called together to unite (NAMES) in Holy matrimony. I begin by asking each of you: are you ready to move into a legally binding relationship, committing yourselves to one another for "as long as you both shall live?" Shall we continue by making pledges, exchanging vows, and giving and receiving rings?

Couple answers together: Yes!

4. (Non-Religious)

Today is different from any other day. Today is the day you will remember for the rest of your lives. This date will be written on application forms, anniversary cards, and party invitations, even years and decades from now. Today is the day that starts the clock ticking on a life-long journey of love that will define both of your lives and create a new and loving family. On this day, are you prepared to bind your lives together in love, rejoicing in the blessings of mutual respect and care?

Couple answers together: We are!

5. (Non-Religious)

(NAMES), having come this far, having planned this event by choosing the words, including the vows you have chosen, and having cared for the legal requirements necessary, are you prepared to join together in marriage by exchanging vows and rings?

Couple answers: Yes, we are ready to be joined together as a married couple and to share our journey as long as we both shall live.

Then let us proceed!

6.

Today as your friend (and pastor), I charge you both to live lives of mutual love and affection in the days to come. You are bringing your individual personalities to this holy place and weaving them together to create a beautiful tapestry that combines the best of you both. As the years pass, the weaving will continue and the beauty increase. Do you surrender yourselves this day to the blessings of a life shared together?

Couple answers together: We do!

7. (Non-Religious)

We are here in this place because you have invited us. You have said that you plan on spending the rest of your lives together, sharing the joys and sorrows, the highs and the lows, and various complications which life throws at us. Is this still true, and do you want to continue by sharing vows of faithfulness and exchanging rings in the presence of this gathering of family and friends?

Couple answers: Yes, we want to share our moment of public commitment with our family and friends!

Then let us proceed!

8.

(NAMES), great music is created when a soloist combines their voice with another to create harmony. Artistic masterpieces begin with the blending of colors. Poets and musicians work together to create something greater than either of them could produce alone. We are here today to celebrate that you have each discovered the person who makes you complete, who complements your gifts, and who enables you both to be greater than you are by yourselves. It is a blessing that you have found one another, and now you share that blessing with us, your friends and family. Do not value that gift lightly, take your partnership for granted, or withhold your beauty and potential from the world.

9. (Non-Religious)

The congregation has come together! The witnesses are here. The legal preparation has been taken care of. We are ready to have a wedding. Are you, (NAMES), prepared to join yourselves in marriage?

Couple answers together: Yes, we want to be united in a bond of love as long as we both shall live.

10. (For an older couple)

(NAMES): Today your journeys have come together, reaffirming our belief that the best is yet to be. You have both known beauty and kindness in your lives, as well as challenge and heartache. And now, by the grace of God, you have experienced the shelter and protection of one another's arms. Today is your day, this place is your special place, and we are your friends and family here to offer you recognition and support as you bind yourselves to each other in the holy name of Love. Amen.

DECLARATION OF CONSENT

The "Declaration of Consent" is the first step toward the formalization of a marriage. It is a statement of willingness and readiness of both parties to proceed with this act of legal, spiritual, and social importance. In some ways, it is not as important as it was many centuries ago. The safety of tribes and family groups does not come into play as it did in ancient societies. We assume the free will of couples coming to be joined in marriage. Yet, it still can hold a place in today's weddings. It says, "Yes! I am ready to move ahead into this new phase of our relationship."

If one wants to reduce the wedding to its briefest possible form, this section could be eliminated. However, it does hold an important place in the long history of couples making commitments that move them from one family group to a new family. In the presence of family and friends, each member of the couple says, "Yes, this is my choice, and I make it without fear, pressure, or reservation."

Traditional

Groom: Will you have this woman to be your wedded wife, to live together in the holy estate of matrimony? Will you love her, comfort her, honor her, and keep her in sickness and in health, and, forsaking all others, keep you only unto her, so long as you both shall live?

Answer: I Will.

Bride: Will you have this man to be your wedded husband, to live together in the holy estate of matrimony? Will you love him, comfort him, honor him, and keep him in sickness and in health, and, forsaking all others, keep you only unto him, as long as you both shall live?

Answer: I Will.

1. (Non-Religious)

(NAME): Are you ready to open your heart to (NAME), and to accept (NAME) as your life partner? Will you love and support (NAME) through times of difficulty, times of change, and times of stress, and will you be supportive of and faithful to (NAME) for the rest of your life?

Answer: Yes, I will.

(Repeat for second member of wedding party.)

2.

(NAME) and (NAME), marriage is an eternal gift with which God may bless our mortal lives, but in this, as in all things, God does not impose God's will on us, but rather invites us into relationship by our own free will. And so I ask your consent:

(NAME), do you take (NAME)to be your wedded partner in life? Do you offer your life to (NAME) as a gift without cost, asking nothing in return but Love itself? And will you devote yourself to (NAME's) happiness and fulfillment in this life?

Answer: I do, and I will.

(Repeat for second member of wedding party.)

3.

(NAME): Words are always inadequate to express our deepest feelings and thoughts, but they are often all that we have. In this moment, standing before family, friends, and the Lord God, will you pledge yourself to (NAME) for all of your remaining days? Will you give (NAME) your love and support as changes occur, and goals change? Will you be supportive of new directions taken, and new goals sought? And will you strive to be the partner who completes (NAME) as a person and a child of God?

Answer: With God's help I will.

(Repeat for second member of wedding party.)

4.

Love is patient, and Love is kind. And so, marriages are shaped not by haste, obligation, or expectation, but rather by considered and thoughtful self-surrender, one to another. (NAME) and (NAME), I invite you now in the name of God and the presence of these family and friends to declare your consent and readiness to enter into the marriage covenant.

(NAME), do you come to this circle of fellowship at peace in your mind and soul with the vows and commitments you make to (NAME) this day?

Answer: I do.

(Repeat for second person.)

Then let the blessings of love shower upon you as you come to this holy place to pledge your devotion to one another.

5. (Non-Religious)

(NAME): Are you prepared to pledge yourself to (NAME) for the rest of your life? Do you realize that (NAME) will change in many ways, will grow older, will develop his/her own talents, and form opinions that may differ from yours? Can you pledge to move into the unknown future with confidence that together you will be at your best and that love will bind you together?

Answer: Yes, I choose to share my future with (NAME).

(Repeat for second member of wedding party.)

6. (For couples in which one or both spouses have experienced a divorce)

(NAME and NAME), you have come to God's holy place this day to make a new commitment to one another in God's holy name. The journey of life is long, and in former days you have shared your life and love with others. We celebrate the blessings of those days and grieve the pain which caused them to end. Today, however, God is doing a new thing and offering in this moment the chance to bind your life to another in holy marriage.

Do you consent, (NAME), to walk with (NAME) in the days to come, side by side, with an open and trusting heart, that you might know all the blessings prepared for you?

Answer: I do.

(Repeat for second member of wedding party.)

7. (Non-Religious)

(NAME): Do you pledge your consent to join in marriage with (NAME)? Will you give all of your strength, all of your energy, all of your encouragement, and all of your support in other ways to encourage (NAME) to become all that (HE/SHE) is capable of becoming? Will you lift (HIM/HER) up when (HE/SHE) stumbles, give (HIM/HER) confidence when (HE/SHE) is afraid, and be supportive when (HE/SHE) is discouraged? Will you be the one that is always there when a helping hand and a true friend is needed?

Answer: Yes! I will, so help me God.

(Repeat for second member of wedding party.)

8.

(NAME) and (NAME), this is the Day the Lord has made. Let us rejoice and be glad in it. We are here today at your invitation to bear witness to your love. We know you and care for you deeply and wish you the best in the years to come. So that all the world might know the desires of your hearts, we ask you now: Do you come freely to give yourself this day to your partner and friend for as long as you both shall live?

Answer: We do!

Will you lighten one another's burdens and encourage one another in times of trouble?

Answer: We will!

Will you share the light of your love as witnesses to a world in need of hope?

Answer: We will!

Then may God richly bless the acts of love and devotion which you share this day. Amen.

PRESENTATION OF THE COUPLE

In earlier days, the purpose of a marriage was often to establish a bond between two families, consolidate property rights, or secure peace between nations. In those times, the "presentation of the bride" made it clear that the woman was being surrendered by her parents (likely her father) in pursuit of family, proprietary, or political goals that might have nothing to do with the desires of the couple actually getting married. We no longer think of brides (or grooms) as property to be "given away," but as independent moral agents, choosing to offer a life-long commitment to one another. Nonetheless, it is appropriate at the beginning of a marriage to give thanks for the parents, siblings, and even children and friends who have accompanied us through the journey of life to the altar. The ceremonial "presentation of the couple" is a way of reminding us that our families of origin (or other important persons) continue to have a role to play in supporting and encouraging the newly-married couple. It also reminds them that they owe the couple the space and freedom to grow and flourish. Thus, the presentation of the couple is really about letting go so that new life may begin.

Traditional

Who gives this woman to be married to this man?

Person who gives the woman: I do, (or) Her mother and I do.

(Changing views of the rights, independence, and strength of women, combined with cultural acceptance of same-sex marriages, may make this part of the traditional service inappropriate in some cases.)

NOTE: Any of these items of "Presentation" may also be used in connection with the groom. Simply substitute "Groom," for "Bride" at appropriate places.

These questions may be answered by the congregation as a group.

1.

Is there anyone who presents (NAME) and offers to be supportive and helpful as (NAME) enters into this marriage?

The guests who know (NAME) answer: Yes, we stand with (NAME) and offer our support as (NAME) enters this marriage. We offer our blessings and our prayers as (NAME) joins (NAME) in holy matrimony.

This may be repeated with the second member of the couple.

2.

Who presents (NAME) and (NAME) to be married in this house of worship this day?

Answer: We, their parents (or "family members").

Will you continue to love and uphold them in the days to come, offering them both roots and wings as they journey together?

Answer: We will.

And will you hold them in your affections and prayers no matter where their paths may take them?

Answer: God being our help, we will. Amen.

3. (Non-Religious)

Who represents the support system, from which (NAME) comes? Do you offer your continuing support and guidance as (NAME) and (NAME) move into this new level of relationship?

Answer of representative or family: Yes! We present (NAME) with pleasure and with confidence for the future of this marriage.

4.

May the families of this couple rise in body or spirit:

Do you present (NAME) and (NAME) in love this day as they bless one another and enter into holy marriage?

Answer: We do!

Will you offer them both your presence and distance in the days to come: respecting the new family they are creating, while holding them close in days of challenge and adversity?

Answer: We will!

Are you prepared to bless them as they face the days to come?

Answer: We are!

Then may God bless you as well, as these two families are woven together in love by the promises that (NAME) and (NAME) make to one another. Amen.

5. (Non-Religious)

Does anyone represent the family and support group which has helped (NAME) become the person that (NAME) is today?

Answer of family, friend, or other representative of family: I do! (or) Her Mother and I do! (or) We do!

6.

(NAME) and (NAME) come together this day to create a new family; they ask for your blessing and love. Let us present them to God this day by joining our voices in prayer:

The families or congregation in unison: Holy and everlasting One. We present before you (NAME) and (NAME), bone of our bone, flesh of our flesh, spirit of our spirits. We have nurtured them, loved them, and encouraged them. Now by your grace, they have found one another, and for that we are grateful. May they continue to feel our hand on their shoulders as they embrace the new life you have set before them. We honor them in your Holy name. Amen.

7. (Non-Religious)

We do not become mature adults without support from many people. Family is usually the primary support system of children, but others, including friends, help us become strong and independent individuals. Who represents this group of people who made (NAME) and (NAME) the amazing people that they are today?

Answer: I do (or) We do.

8. (For couples who have lost parents to death)
Everlasting God, we gather in the presence of the saints this day, confident that those we have lost to death are eternal in you. Under your holy heaven, we receive the blessings of all who have gone before us as we feel their love and affection even now. We are standing on the shoulders of our beloved ancestors, and we honor them. May this couple know they are presented here this day by all who have loved them and longed for their happiness. Amen.

9. (Non-Religious)

No one reaches the point where he or she is ready to enter into a long-term committed relationship like marriage without the support and strength of family and friends. Is there a representative of the family or circle of friends of (NAME) who presents (HIM/HER) before this congregation?

Answer: I do (or) We do.

(Repeat for second member.)

SCRIPTURE READINGS

Weddings that join Christians, Jews, or other people of faith together "in Holy Matrimony" often include words from the scripture of their religion as part of the ceremony. There is no rule that requires readings from the Bible, Koran, or other holy book, but it can make the service more meaningful for the participants and/or those gathered to witness the wedding.

Throughout history, certain bits of literature have lifted the spirits of those who have read or heard them. The Bible, the Koran, and other writings connected with religious groups have been at the top of the list of "inspirational texts." Such words of inspiration may add to your wedding. They are not mandatory, but it is worth considering if you, your family, or other guests will be uplifted by including them.

In an effort to make it easier for you, we have made some recommendations that have been used at weddings at which we have officiated, or are suggested as good possibilities for Christian or Jewish weddings. We do not have suggestions for Muslim weddings, but suspect that any Muslim officiants would have access to such readings.

Old Testament Readings

Genesis 1:26 – 31 "And God said, "Let us make man in our image..."

Genesis 2:18 – 25 "Then the Lord God said, "It is not good..."

Psalm 67 "May God be gracious to us..."

Psalm 127 "Unless the Lord builds the house..."

Psalm 134 "Come, bless the Lord..."

Jeremiah 31:31 – 34 "Behold, the days are coming..."

New Testament Readings

Romans 12:1 – 3, 9 – 13 "I appeal to you therefore…"

1 Corinthians 13:4 – 8a "Now there are varieties of
gifts…"

Ephesians 3:14 – 21 "For this reason I bow my knees…"

Colossians 3:12 – 17 "Put on then, as God's chosen ones…"

I John 4:7 – 12 "Beloved, let us love one another…"

Matthew 5:2 – 4 "And he opened his mouth and taught
them…"

Matthew 7:24-29 "Everyone then, who hears these words
of mine…"

Matthew 19:4 – 6 "He answered, Have you not read that
he who made them…"

Matthew 22:35 – 40 "And one of them, a lawyer, asked
him a question…"

John 2:1 – 11 "On the third day there was a marriage at
Cana…"

John 15:11 – 17 "These things I have spoken to you…

Exchange of Vows

The "Exchange of Vows" is the heart of the wedding. The simplicity or complexity of the vows may vary from person to person, but the essence of the wedding is found in whatever statement which is chosen to say, "Yes, I choose you!" These are the words that satisfy the legal requirement for a wedding.

This is also the moment in the wedding when the couple has the opportunity to express themselves regarding their love and commitment to one another. Most couples don't know much about weddings, but they do know that somewhere in the religious or civil ceremony they get to say, "I Do!" Those two words may be the only thing that a couple knows about weddings. The "vows" are an expansion of those two words.

The choice of one or more of the "vows" offered in the following pages, or any combination of those vows, can be improved if the participants add personal notes or memories to the words chosen. We encourage you to consider memorizing your vows, or perhaps printing them on cards so that you can share them without the officiant breaking them into small phrases to be repeated. We also encourage you to consider choosing your vows based on what you want to say to your marriage partner. The vows of both partners do not need to be the same. Feel free to choose or create words which express your love and commitment to the person that you are marrying.

The following suggestions are offered with the hope that they may stimulate you to think about your own words of commitment to one another. Please note that both members of the wedding couple do not need to use the same vow. It may be that one of you feels drawn to one set of words and the other person is better represented by another set of words. Best of all, we encourage you to create your own vows. The words here (and those found in the "Renewal of Vows" section) may stimulate you to come up with new words that better represent your feelings and commitment to your life partner. Be creative!

Traditional

Officiant: Repeat after me:

"I (NAME) take you (NAME) to be my wedded (wife, husband, partner), to have and to hold, from this day forward, for better, for worse, for richer, for poorer, in sickness and in health, to love and to cherish, till death us do part, according to God's holy ordinance; and thereto I pledge thee my faith."

1.

Officiant: Repeat after me:

"(NAME), I am thrilled and delighted to tell you and the world how much I love you. My world has changed since I met you. You have given me a reason to smile. You have filled my heart with love and joy. And, you have made every day a day filled with promise and fulfillment.

"I take this opportunity to commit myself to share the journey with you for the rest of our lives. I will walk with you on the uncertain paths of life. I will give you my support and affection in every way that I can. Your dreams will become my dreams, and our home will be a place of peace and love."

(This or another "vow" may be offered by the second member of the wedding couple.)

2.

Officiant: (NAME), take (NAME) by your hand, and repeat after me...

(NAME), this day we join our hearts as well as our hands.

In your presence, I am made whole.

I am at peace by your side today,

And I will remain there, so long as we both shall live.

This is my sacred pledge.

(This or another "vow" may be offered by the second member of the wedding couple.)

3.

Officiant: Repeat after me:

"(NAME) This is the day that we have dreamed about. Since we met and our love began to flourish, I have hoped and prayed that we could be joined together in a covenant of love. Thus, I, (NAME), take you, (NAME), to be my (husband, wife, chosen partner) for as long as we live. I give you my lifelong love, my respect, and my trust. I will never abandon or forsake you, so help me God."

(This or another "vow" may be offered by the second member of the wedding couple.)

4.

Officiant: Vows are promises, but they are bigger than that. Vows are promises made in the presence of God and our gathered family and community. They are public promises that invite the support and encouragement of all who care for us. Together we surround this couple with our prayers and good intentions as they make their vows to one another.

(NAME) and (NAME), I invite you to repeat these words you have chosen as expressions of your love.

(NAME), I give my whole self to you today,

My body and soul, my hopes and dreams.

I choose you above all others

And in your arms, I have found my home.

May the Ancient One bear witness to our pledge,

And watch over us in the days to come.

Amen.

(This or another "vow" may be offered by the second member of the wedding couple.)

5.

Officiant: Repeat after me:

"I, (NAME), take you, (NAME), to be my (life partner, husband, wife). I will be your friend, your support, and your helper as long as we both shall live. I pledge my love to you, and to you only, as long as we both shall live. I offer my gifts, my strength, my patience, and my vulnerability to you, as long as we both shall live. I promise to honor you in every way that I can. I offer these words in the holy name of God."

(This or another "vow" may be offered by the second member of the wedding couple.)

6.

Officiant: (NAME) and (NAME), you come together on this date which will become a milestone on the roads that both of you will travel. We are here to witness and support your public profession of love, as your two journeys become one.

I invite you to speak these words by which you are united:

(NAME), today I stand with open hands and open heart, and choose you as my own.

I will travel with you

In good times and in bad,

I celebrate all that you have given me, to make me who I am.

I take you as my spouse and partner for life. Here and now. I publicly pledge my love to you.

(This or another "vow" may be offered by the second member of the wedding couple.)

7.

Officiant: Repeat after me:

"(NAME), this is the moment I have prayed for ever since we met. I truly believe that God created us to be together. Therefore, I, (NAME), take you (NAME), to be my (life partner, husband, wife) so long as we both shall live. I offer myself without reservation, to love, honor and cherish you, through sickness and health, through good times and times of stress. I will be your partner no matter what life will bring. This is my vow, in the Holy name of God."

(This or another "vow" may be offered by the second member of the wedding couple.)

8. (Vows made in dialogue)

Officiant: Today, (NAME) and (NAME), I invite you to make your vow of love to one another:

Today I am yours

And I am yours

Today we join our hands

And our hearts

And create a family

A union of our spirits

No matter what trials may come

We are one.

In days of health and joy

We will celebrate one another

And in days of sickness or adversity

We will care for one another.

Around us

We draw a circle of devotion and protection.

I take you as my [wife/husband/spouse]

And I take you as my [wife/husband/spouse]

To have and to hold

From this day forward

[With one voice]: **Together as one. Amen.**

9.

Officiant: Repeat after me:

"(NAME) for (number of months or years) we have shared our journey. Our lives have been intertwined, and I can't imagine living without you by my side. I am not complete without you. I love you, and I want to share my journey with you for as long as we both shall live.

"I take you as my love, my friend, and my partner, for all the days to come. God is my witness."

(This or another "vow" may be offered by the second member of the wedding couple.)

Exchange of Rings

A simple metal band worn on the third finger (on either the right or left hand) is an international symbol of a man or a woman in a committed relationship. The presentation and acceptance of these symbols is often one of the highlights of the wedding ceremony. Rings are not required, are sometimes only worn by one member of the married couple, and are occasionally left out of the wedding ceremony. However, they are normally part of weddings as we experience them.

The circle, without beginning or end, has long been a symbol of love, and in particular of the love of God. The fact that wedding rings are often made of silver or gold is of no special significance, except that they are of value in more than one way. While many couples have "matching" wedding rings, there is no need for this to be the case. The ring is simply an outward and visible sign of in inward and spiritual relationship.

Traditional

Officiant: Let us pray. Bless, O Lord, the giving of these rings, that they who wear them may abide in thy peace, and continue in thy favor; through Jesus Christ our Lord. Amen.

Groom: In token and pledge of our constant faith and abiding love, with this ring I thee wed, in the name of the Father, and of the Son, and of the Holy Spirit. Amen.

Bride: In token and pledge of our constant faith and abiding love, with this ring I thee wed, in the name of the Father, and of the Son, and of the Holy Spirit. Amen.

1.

Officiant: I hold in my hand two rings which will soon be exchanged and worn by (NAME and NAME). The rings are symbols of their commitment to one another. But beyond that, they are also symbols of a relationship, which, like a circle, will never end. There is no weak spot in a circle. It just goes on forever. Love endures when everything else falls away. These rings are symbols of everlasting love. May they be constant reminders that you are loved by one another and by God.

(NAME), place the ring on (NAME'S) finger and repeat after me:

"I give you this ring with the promise that as long as I live my love for you will never end."

(Repeat with second member of wedding couple.)

2.

Officiant: Wedding rings are circles, universal symbols of strength and eternity. Made of precious metals, something we highly prize here on earth, they remind us that by giving ourselves in love to others, we build up treasures in heaven. As (NAME and NAME) make the highest of all commitments today, may these rings be blessed reminders that (NAME and NAME) are held in love by the One who created them, today and every day. Amen.

Repeat after me:

"(NAME), I give you this ring and offer you my love as a symbol of my enduring devotion, in the name of [God] or [the Father, Son, and Holy Spirit] or [the Creator, Redeemer, and Sustainer]. Amen."

3. (Non-Religious)

Officiant: The wedding ring symbolizes the connection which two people have with one another. It reminds us of never-ending commitment to one another. With no end, a circle is a symbol of continuity, and of love enduring forever.

(NAME), does this ring represent your enduring commitment to (NAME), and do you pledge to honor (NAME) as long as you both shall live?

Answer: "I Do!" (*placing ring on finger of spouse*)

(Repeat with second member of wedding couple.)

4.

Let us pray:

Holy and beloved Creator, we set aside these symbols taken from deep in the earth as reminders of your blessed, loving kindness. When (NAME and NAME) see and cherish these rings, may they be reminded that they themselves are cherished by you, and by all who gather here today. AMEN.

(NAME), receive this ring and treasure it,
Accept my body as your own,
my breath as your breath,
And receive my love as I freely offer it to you this day.
Amen.

5.

Officiant: It would be nice if you could give your (loving partner, best friend, spouse) a beautiful bouquet or a fabulous jacket, or some other symbol which would remind (THEM) that you love (THEM). But such a gift would whither, or wear out, or could become burdensome. A ring is a tried and true symbol of God's everlasting love and of the love of two people for one another. Thus, (NAME AND NAME) are exchanging rings to declare to the world that each of them has chosen their special partner.

Repeat after me as you place the ring on (HIS/HER) finger:

"I give you this ring as a symbol of my never-ending love for you. I am committed to loving you forever. I will use all my strength to care for you, to protect you, and to make you happy, so help me God."

(Repeat with second member of wedding couple.)

6.

Human beings raise up great monuments so that we will remember important moments in history or influential leaders. These objects derive meaning from that which they symbolize. Today, (NAME and NAME) give rings to one another. They are beautifully made, but their importance lies in what they stand for: a love that is durable, mature, self-sacrificing, and eternal. May they who share such powerful symbols be blessed by God to be a blessing to all of us.

(NAME), I give you this ring as a symbol of my enduring love and devotion. I cherish you above all others, and my home will always be with you. Amen.

7. (Non-Religious)

Officiant: The wedding ring has long been a symbol of the commitment made by two people. Most wedding rings are simple, plain gold bands, that identify people in committed relationships. (You may add a description of the rings). (NAME and NAME), do these rings symbolize your commitment to one another?

Couple: They do!

Officiant to first member of couple: As you place the ring on your loved one's hand, repeat after me:

"With this ring I symbolize my enduring love for you, and my commitment to be true and faithful to you for the rest of my life."

(Repeat with second member of wedding couple.)

8. (For couples who have previous children)

As written, this liturgy includes the giving of symbols to the stepchildren of the couple. Such symbols might be necklaces, pins, bracelets, or other item of significance.

Officiant: Today, we celebrate Love, the love of spouses but also the love of (NAME and NAME's) new family. Let us bless these rings [and/or symbols] of this love that are shared between (NAME and NAME) and with their children... Let us pray:

Holy and Eternal God, who loves us as parents love their children, may these holy symbols remind us of the new bonds of love and affection that are woven today between the members of this new family. Bless they who wear them, and remind each of them that they are precious in your eyes. Amen.

Spouse to spouse:

(NAME), I give you this ring [and/or symbol] as a token of my enduring love, and pledge to uphold you in all your life's journey. You complete me, and for that I am forever grateful.

Spouses to their new stepchildren:

(NAME), today we are connected by our mutual love for your (mother/father). As I treasure (him/her), so will I treasure you, and I give you this symbol of our new relationship. May God watch over us as we grow together as a family. Amen.

9.

Officiant: I hold the wedding ring(s) in my hand. They are simple pieces of jewelry that represent an extraordinarily complex relationship between two people drawn together by God's love. It will last for hundreds or even thousands of years. Some of us still have our parents' weddings rings. Museums display the wedding rings of famous people of history. We only ask and pray for these rings to symbolize a relationship that will last seventy-five or one hundred years. May God bless the rings, and more especially those who will wear them. Amen!

Repeat after me as you place the ring on your loved one's finger:

"With this ring I symbolize my love for you. I will celebrate that love as long as we both shall live."

(Repeat with second member of wedding couple.)

10.

Officiant: (NAME) and (NAME), I invite you to share your vows, using the words of ancient Scripture.

(NAME), wherever you go, I will go;
wherever you live, I will live.
Your people will be my people,
and your God will be my God.
Today I take you as my [wife, husband, spouse, partner],
And pledge my life-long love to you.
Amen.

(This or another "vow" may be offered by the second member of the wedding couple.)

PRONOUNCEMENT OR DECLARATION

When the officiant has witnessed the completion of the process of two people making a binding legal agreement to be one family, the Pronouncement or Declaration tells the world that a legal and/or spiritual commitment has been made. With these words he/she offers a concluding statement such as: "It is done! They are now partners in the journey of life. Their lives are connected, and they are officially a family!"

The Pronouncement/Declaration does not necessarily end the wedding. Prayers, Affirmations of those present, music, and blessings may follow the official statement of completion. Whatever happens next, however, happens after the couple is actually married. It is now a celebration!

Traditional

Forasmuch as (NAME and NAME) have consented together in holy wedlock, and have witnessed the same before God and this company, and thereto have pledged their faith each to the other, and have declared the same by joining hands and by giving and receiving rings; I pronounce that they are husband and wife together, in the name of the Father, and of the Son, and of the Holy Spirit. Those whom God hath joined together, let no one put asunder. Amen.

1.

We have witnessed a sacred moment today. (FULL NAME and FULL NAME) have declared their love for one another. They have exchanged vows of commitment (as well as given and received rings), and God being our witness, I now declare that they are (husband and wife, life partners, a married couple, committed to one another) for as long as they both shall live. Let us offer our love and support to them as they travel the complicated and uncertain path of every relationship.

2.

(NAME) and (NAME), you have brought joy to us this day. You have spoken words of love, exchanged symbols of commitment, and taken vows of devotion. In the eyes of God, this community, and your families, you are united in marriage. God bless you both!

3.

We have witnessed a sacred moment today. (FULL NAME and FULL NAME) have declared their love for one another. They have exchanged vows of commitment (as well as given and received rings), and God being our witness, I now declare that they are (husband and wife, life partners, a married couple, committed to one another) for as long as they both shall live.

4. (Non-Religious)

It seems so simple: people gather, words are said, gifts are given, and promises are made. But all things of beauty are born in simplicity, and now these beautiful lives are united in one. It is my privilege and honor this day to declare you both well and truly married.

5.

God has created us to be together. Today, (NAME and NAME) have committed themselves to be joined in a holy marriage. They have chosen to place the God of love and grace at the center of their life together. We have witnessed a covenant between two people that we love, and the God who created us all. They are now joined together in holy matrimony. We celebrate their love and commitment to God as well as to one another.

6.

Upon this sacred ground, within this holy space, two of God's children have spoken their vows and pledged their love. We are witnesses, as are the heavens under which we gather. I declare to you that they are married, united by their promises and devotion, one to the other. Amen.

7.

By the authority which has been given to me by the (NAME OF CHURCH) and the State of ______________, I declare to you that (NAME and NAME) are now married by the Church and the State. They have exchanged words of love and commitment, and have chosen to share the journey of life with one another. May God continue to bless them as they share that journey in the years to come.

8. (Non-Religious)

Today, lives are united, spirits are joined, love is alive, and hope is reborn. Can anything be more satisfying than to declare these two lovely spirits united in marriage? May they inspire us as they continue to give themselves to one another in selfless love for the rest of their days. Amen.

9.

We have heard the words spoken by (NAME and NAME). They have declared their love for one another, pledged their faithfulness to one another, and promised to support and care for one another in the days and years to come. Thus, they have chosen to be married according to the laws of the State of ______________. As a representative of the State, I declare to you that they are duly married. May God bless them in their journey together.

10.

Today the love given to each of you from above is reflected in this sacred ritual. We have not only confirmed what God has already done in your lives, but what a joy it is to stand beside you this days and to declare you married in the eyes of your Creator and your community. Amen.

WEDDING PRAYERS

In the Wedding ceremony, some of the words are directed to the gathered community by the officiant and some to the couple themselves. Other words are spoken by the persons getting married to one another. Still other words are addressed from the community to the couple. The Wedding Prayer, however, is directed toward God. Even though the officiant is talking to God, he or she is also talking about God to those who overhear the prayer. It is appropriate to ask for God's direction and blessing for the marriage being celebrated, not because God needs to be reminded, but because the couple may have forgotten that their heavenly companion will always accompany them.

Traditional

O eternal God, creator and preserver of all, giver of all spiritual grace, the author of everlasting life: Send thy blessing upon this man and woman, whom we bless in thy name, that they may surely perform and keep the vow and covenant between them made, and may ever remain in perfect love and peace together, and live according to your laws. Look graciously upon them, that they may love, honor, and cherish each other, and so live together in faithfulness and patience, in wisdom and true godliness, that their home may be a haven of blessing and a place of peace; Through Jesus Christ our Lord. Amen.

1.

Let us pray:

God of love and grace, we turn to you as our friends have shared their pledges of love, each to the other. We celebrate the love which you have given to all of us, and our ability to share that love with one another. Bless (NAME and NAME) as they have affirmed their love for each other and as they seek to live within the context of your love for them. May that love be reflected in the way that they act toward one another (as well as toward all their children), and the way that they act toward all humanity. We pray that their lives, and their life together as a family, may be a model for others as together we seek to serve you. Amen.

2.

Gracious and Holy Creator, in this space, persons have spoken holy, sacred words binding them one to another. We have witnessed the making of covenant here, we have offered our affirmation and support, we have celebrated with the exchange of rings. Now, as we prepare to receive (NAME and NAME) as married members of our community, we ask you to bless them with happiness, mutual support, kindness, and understanding. May they be a blessing to one another and to us, and we give thanks for you bringing them together. Amen.

3.

Will you join me as we pray for (NAME and NAME).

Lord, this is a day of celebration for us. We celebrate the love which (NAME and NAME) have declared in our midst. We celebrate the love which is reflected by members of this gathered group. We celebrate the love which you have given to us through your amazing creation, through the whole human family, and especially through these two friends who share their promises with us. May your love be reflected in the way they live with one another (and with their children), as well as the way they treat friends and strangers alike. Bless (NAME and NAME) in their journey. Grant them enduring love, peace, and joy. We ask in the name of Jesus, the Christ. Amen.

4.

And now faith, hope, and love abide, these three. And the greatest of these is love.

Let us pray:

Holy One, today we celebrate the marriage of (NAME and NAME) and ask that your strength and compassion be the watchwords of their relationship. Help them to defend one another from the challenges of life, rejoice with one another in days of happiness, and grow old with one another in security and serenity. We thank you for the gifts of marriage, life, and companionship, and we thank you for the blessed example of this couple who have pledged themselves to one another this day. Amen.

5.

Join me as we pray God's blessing on (NAME and NAME).

God of love, we turn to you with grateful hearts as we have witnessed words and acts of love shared today. We celebrate the love which (NAME and NAME) have found in each other. May their act of love remind us of the love which we share with others: partners, family members, neighbors, friends, coworkers, and even strangers. Let love be the most important part of every day and every relationship. We accept your love with gratitude and humility. Help us to reflect that love as we interact with one another. Amen.

6.

Holy God, it is not in our nature to put others before ourselves. Rather we tend to be a people of self-interest and obsession. But not today! Today we celebrate and lift into your heavenly light (NAME and NAME), who have put one another first in their hearts. They remind us that we are stronger when we are woven together, whether in marriage, friendship, or faith. Help us grow toward that ideal and bless this couple who have celebrated their shared journey on this, their wedding day. Thank you for helping them to find one another, to know one another, and to commit to one another in love. Amen.

7.

Let us pray:

This is a day which the Lord has made! Let us rejoice and be glad in it! Lord, we do rejoice as we celebrate the shared love which has been symbolized by (NAME and NAME) exchanging vows (and rings) in our presence. Thank you for creating us in such a way that we can love one another. Help us to expand our circle of love so that others will see your love through our words and actions. We pray your special blessing on (NAME and NAME) (and their children), whom we bless in your name. May their journey be filled with love, and their lives be testimonies of your grace. Amen.

8. (For blended families)

Holy God, our lives are complex things, woven of circumstance, decisions, and risk. It can be difficult to find you among the many events of everyday life. But today we stop, place our feet on solid ground, and feel your sunshine of blessing on our faces. Today, two families have been woven into one; two histories and two futures have been united. May you watch over all who are brought into new relationships this day: Not only (NAME and NAME) who have pledged themselves to each other, but parents-in-law, brothers and sisters-in-law, step-siblings, cousins, and so many more [*modify as appropriate*]. Today's holy ceremony reminds us that we are all one human family, and that the joys and sorrows of any one of us belong to us all. Thank you for bringing us together, and may your grace accompany us all in days to come. Amen.

9.

Let us pray:

Love fills this place today, Lord! We saw it as we watched (NAME and NAME) look at one another. We saw it as we listened to their exchange of vows (and watched the giving and receiving of rings). And we now we see it as we enjoy family and friends being supportive and celebrating what is happening in our midst.

Love fills this place today, Lord! And we know that it is a reflection of your love for us. We thank you for allowing us to love you and to love one another. May we continue to reflect your love in all our relationships. We ask these things in the name of Jesus. Amen.

10 (For couples from different faith traditions)

Gracious and holy God, God of Abraham and Sarah, (God of Muhammed), (God known to us through Jesus), God of saints and sinners, today (NAME and NAME) have come together and embraced their most sacred traditions as they have pledged their lives to each other. They bring different beliefs, different experiences, and different stories to this sacred place, but they are now united in one Love. May their unity in diversity give hope to us all, and may the world be a better place because of the love that they share and the example that they give. May it be so.

THE LORD'S PRAYER

The Lord's Prayer is by far the best known prayer in the Christian Church. It is believed to have been prayed by Jesus and to be a model for the prayers of those who follow the teachings of Jesus. Jesus is reported to have said, "When you pray, pray like this." The Lord's prayer followed that word of instruction.

Some Christian Churches use the word "debts" at one point in the prayer, while other Christian Churches use the word "trespasses." The meaning is essentially the same. The intent at that point in the prayer is "forgive us, as we forgive others."

Occasionally the Lord's Prayer follows the wedding prayer. This provides an opportunity for those present to participate in a prayer for the married couple. If a bulletin or "order of service" is distributed prior to the wedding, it can be helpful to indicate whether "debts" or "trespasses" is to be used.

A modern version of the Lord's Prayer

Holy creator of all that is, Your name is holy. May Your Kingdom be discovered among us, and may Your hope for humanity and creation be fulfilled soon. May Your wishes for your human family be realized in our time.

We ask for our needs, and those of all creation, to be met today. Even more, we ask for our spiritual needs be met. Forgive our sins, our poor decisions, our selfish acts, as we forgive the same acts of others against us and against your creation.

Help us to avoid places and people which will tempt us to make bad decisions and to push us away from You. Keep us safe from evil and make us conscious of Your presence.

We acknowledge that everything on earth and in heaven is under Your authority, and all power and glory belongs to you. Amen!

The Lord's Prayer using "Debts"

Our Father, who art in heaven, hallowed be thy name. Thy kingdom come. Thy will be done, on earth as it is in heaven. Give us this day our daily bread. And forgive us our debts as we forgive our debtors. And lead us not into temptation, but deliver us from evil. For thine is the kingdom and the power, and the glory forever. Amen!

The Lord's Prayer using "Trespasses"

Our Father, who art in heaven, hallowed be thy name. Thy kingdom come. Thy will be done, on earth as it is in heaven. Give us this day our daily bread. And forgive us our trespasses as we forgive those who trespass against us. And lead us not into temptation, but deliver us from evil. For thine is the kingdom and the power, and the glory forever. Amen!

AFFIRMATIONS OF THE COMMUNITY

Parents and family do not cease to be a part of the married couple's life on the day of the wedding. Neither does their wider community of friends and companions. The "affirmation of the community" is an opportunity for all to declare their support of the new family that has been created. It also allows the community to offer help and respect the couple's independence and privacy. A wedding is not a "spectator sport." Those who attend have a role to play on the day of the ceremony, as well as in days to come. Their role begins with a heartfelt and robust affirmation of these two lives, now joined together.

1.

Officiant: Will you join with me as we offer words of affirmation and support to (NAME and NAME)?

Congregation: We join our voices in celebration of the marriage of (NAME and NAME). We offer them our support as they grow together, as they change through the coming years, and as they continue to become the people that you want them to be. May the joy of this moment last for all of their lives.

2.

Officiant: Friends and Family of (NAME and NAME), do you pledge your support to the family created here today?

 Congregation: WE DO!

 Officiant: Will you stand by them in good times and bad, offer them your love, and give them space to grow together?

 Congregation: WE WILL!

 Officiant: Then surely (NAME and NAME) will never stand alone. Thanks be to God.

 Congregation: AMEN!

3.

Officiant: I invite you to offer words of support and affirmation to (NAME and NAME) as they begin their lives as a married couple.

Congregation: (NAME and NAME), we offer our support as you begin life as a married couple. We join in your joy and celebrate with you the committed relationship which you have confirmed in our presence. May God bless you today, and for the rest of your lives together. And may you discover new joy in your journey as husband and wife.

4.

Officiant: The beautiful music of these vows seeks an echo in the lives of you, the family and friends of (NAME and NAME). May they know your love and support all the days of their marriage.

Congregation: They will, we promise this day!

5.

Officiant: Let us join as one voice as we acknowledge and celebrate the wedding which we have just witnessed.

Congregation: (NAME and NAME), you have declared before God and all of us that you have chosen one another to share your journey with for the years to come. We celebrate your decision and pledge our support and friendship to help you through whatever challenges or hard decisions lie ahead. We love you and offer our prayers to keep you close to God and one another.

6.

Officiant: Married life is a journey, and not every day is easy. (NAME and NAME) ask for and will need your affirmation and support. Will you who celebrate with them today uphold them in joy and sorrow, heartache and victory?

Congregation: WE WILL!

Officiant: May God who gives you the will to say these things, also give you the strength to do them.

Congregation: AMEN!

7.

Officiant: Friends, you have witnessed an important moment in the lives of (NAME and NAME).

Do you pledge to encourage and support (NAME and NAME) as they share the coming years?

Congregation: WE DO!

Officiant: Do you commit yourself to pray for (NAME and NAME) as they share their faith journey as well as their lives as (husband and wife, spouses, partners, etc.)?

Congregation: WE DO!

Officiant: And finally, do you offer to be of assistance in any ways that you can when problems arise and support is needed?

Congregation: WE DO!

8. (Non-Religious)

We are gathered together as a spiritual village this day to affirm, bless, and encourage (NAME and NAME) in their new life.

[optional] Will you form a circle around them, joining hearts and hands together?

Let all who bless them today repeat after me:

(NAME and NAME), we stand with you this day...

Holding you in our hearts...

Blessing you with our hopes and dreams...

And encouraging you with our voices...

You belong to us...

And we will not let you go...

Amen!

9. (Non-Religious)

The vows have been taken. The rings have been given and received. Soon the documents will be signed, and the State will be notified. A wedding has taken place.

And we are witnesses of this event. If you wish to affirm this wedding, to celebrate this wedding, or to offer your love to this couple, you may do so with your applause.

(The congregation may applaud!)

10. (For a blended family)

Officiant: Today, two families have become one, and (NAME and NAME) ask for your blessing and support.

(NAME 1's family), do you welcome and accept (NAME 2) into your household of love? Do you promise to support, love, and nurture (HIM/HER) as a part of your family circle? And will you cherish (HIM/HER) as God's gift to you all?

Congregation: WE DO AND WE WILL!

Officiant: And (NAME 2's family), do you welcome and accept (NAME 1) into your household of love? Do you promise to support, love, and nurture (HIM/HER) as a part of your family circle? And will you cherish (HIM/HER) as God's gift to you all?

Congregation: WE DO AND WE WILL!

All: AMEN.

Closing Prayers and Benedictions

When the wedding ends, the marriage begins. In a similar fashion, when the wedding ceremony concludes, those present move from a formal setting of commitment into the daily realities of life. Suddenly we leave the church, or the setting of the wedding, and are confronted by friends, family, and strangers alike.

The Benediction, or Blessing, is a brief, simple word that takes place at the end of any Christian worship service, as well as at most—if not all—other religious gatherings. That word sends those present back into the world knowing that they are not alone. God accompanies them as they face hardships, experience great joys, and live life with all of its ups and downs. Simple words such as "Go in Peace, and the Peace of God go with you" remind those present that God is with them. They carry a blessing with them as they move from a holy moment into a secular world.

Both the newly-married couple and the guests who have witnessed the marriage can benefit from a good word that surrounds and empowers their re-engagement with our secular world. The Benediction is a liturgical way of saying: Life can be difficult. Know that you are not alone. God is with you!

Traditional

God, the Father, the Son, and the Holy Spirit bless, preserve, and keep you; the Lord graciously with his favor look upon you, and so fill you with all spiritual benediction and love that you may so live together in this life that in the world to come you may have life everlasting. Amen.

1.

Let us pray: God of all creation, we offer our thanks, especially for enabling us to establish lasting, committed relationships with one another. Our worship today has celebrated the commitment of (NAME and NAME) to one another. We rejoice that they found one another, that they have allowed themselves to love one another, and that they have pledged themselves to one another in this wedding. We ask you to bless this marriage, to enfold these friends, your children, in your love, and to let their lives demonstrate your love for all people. May all of us be witnesses of love and grace to all humanity. Amen.

2.

Gracious God, protect this couple as they go out into the world. Let all creation know that a family has been born this day, a family meant for the blessing of their neighbors as well as for your glory. We greet them today, we will walk with them tomorrow, and we rejoice in our friendship and mutual love. Amen.

3.

Let us pray: Loving God, you have given us the ability to love one another. More than that, you have instructed us to share your love. Our worship today has been an affirmation of love in our midst. We thank you for the witness that (NAME and NAME) have shared with us. Help us to be living examples as we leave this place, that others may see your love through our words and actions. We ask this in the name of Jesus, our Christ. Amen.

4.

Rejoice brothers and sisters, mothers and fathers, children and elders. Today, (NAME and NAME) have become one. May we be blessed by their mutual love, inspired by their union, and encouraged by their example. We have been blessed to be witnesses and we place our prayers for their happiness upon this altar. Amen.

5.

Let us pray: We offer our gratitude for your presence among us, Lord. We have witnessed a symbol of your love for us and for all your people. (NAME and NAME) have pledged their love, and have committed themselves to sharing their journey of faith. May this commitment be evident within each of us. May our lives reflect your love by our words and actions in the coming days and years. Help us to be faithful to your will for us and all humanity. We ask these things in the name and spirit of Jesus. Amen.

6.

(NAME and NAME), I rest my hands upon your hands and bid you go with God from this holy place. You carry the benediction of the Almighty upon your souls, and the prayers of this community upon your marriage. You could not be better prepared for the days to come. So travel in peace to the places God will lead you and always remember this day and the blessings of this congregation. Amen.

7.

Let us pray: Thank you for your grace and your love, Lord. May we leave this service committed to be Your people in a troubled world. Help us to be instruments of love, offering ourselves to help others, and make our world a better place. We ask this in the name of Jesus, the Christ. Amen.

8. (Non-Religious)

(NAME and NAME),
> The warmth of summer nourish you,
> The colors of autumn inspire you,
> The deep snows of winter draw you closer to one another,
> And the blossoming of spring renew your spirits.
> We bless you for all the days to come. Amen.

9.

Let us pray: Thank you for the privilege of witnessing this service of commitment and love, Lord. We are uplifted as we see and hear (NAME and NAME) commit themselves to one another. Help us to reflect this level of love in our interactions with others. May our family, our friends, and even strangers discover your love through our words and actions. Furthermore, may we be aware of your presence moment by moment as we continue to be your people building the kingdom of God on earth, as it is in heaven. Amen.

10. (Non-Religious)

(NAME and NAME), you have chosen to walk the rest of your days by one another's side. We cannot know the journey you will travel, but we know that you will bless and strengthen one another. May happiness be your path and may your trust in one another guide you to a place of peace. Amen.

11. (Non-Religious)

We have witnessed the sharing of a covenant. Two friends have made promises and declared before us and the world that they choose each other. Now we offer words of blessing to them. The wedding ceremony ends, but the marriage begins. We, family and friends, seek to encourage, support, and love you as together you create your own future. May love abound as life continues. Amen.

12.

Go in Peace, and may the peace of God go with you. Amen.

Special Services

Renewal of Vows

As mentioned in the "For Your Consideration" section, the renewal of wedding vows can be very meaningful.

A service of renewal can be as simple or complex as you wish. All of the choices available for weddings may be adapted to create a service of renewal that meets your needs and desires. By simply adding or deleting words here and there (as is evident in the first offering listed on the next page), you can easily use almost any part of the words found in the section on "wedding vows" to restate your affection and commitment to one another.

In an effort to make it easier for you, we offer the following words as substitutes for the wedding vows. Do not feel limited to choosing only one of these possibilities. It is entirely possible that the first person can use one vow, and the second person can use a different vow. The vows should reflect what you feel and what you want to express.

1.

Officiant: Repeat after me:

"I said it before, and now I say it again. I, (NAME), take you, (NAME), to be my wedded (wife, husband, spouse), to have and to hold, from this day forward, for better, for worse, for richer, for poorer, in sickness and in health, to love and to cherish, 'til death us do part, according to God's holy ordinance; and thereto I pledge thee my faith."

(Repeat with second member of the married couple.)

2.

My dearest (NAME), words cannot express what you have meant to me: before we were married, on the day of our wedding, and every day since! How wonderful that I get to tell you, and all of our friends and family, that I chose you then, I choose you now, and I will always choose you to walk by my side and share my life. I pledge myself to you once again. I am yours for as long as we both shall live.

(Repeat with second member of the married couple.)

3.

Officiant: Repeat after me:

"(NAME), I don't have enough words to tell you how much you mean to me, how much the past (number of years married) years have meant to me. I told you then that I loved you and was committed to be with you as long as we both shall live. I renew that vow today. But I do so with the experience of spending (number of years married) years with you. I have watched you grow as I have grown. I have been blessed by your love, even as I have loved you. And I have discovered talents and gifts which you have shared with me for all these years. I take this opportunity to tell you once again that I love you, and I want to spend the rest of my life with you."

(Repeat with second member of the married couple.)

4.

First partner: (NAME), together we have withstood the test of time. We have survived good times and bad, chaos and quiet, worry and contentment, challenge and fear. No matter what, we have been here for one another. And today we pledge to each other that our story will continue.

Second partner: (NAME), we cannot know what the future will bring, but today we share with all who love us that we will face that future together, you and me, side by side, for as long as we both shall live.

First partner: (NAME), I renew my vow of marriage, and once again take you as my (husband/wife/spouse).

Second partner: (NAME), I renew my vow of marriage, and once again take you as my (husband/wife/spouse).

Together: May the God who brought us together keep us together, so that we may be a blessing to each other and an example of love.

5.

Officiant to first person: Repeat after me:

"(NAME), I told you (number of years married) years ago that I loved you and was committed to sharing my life with you. Nothing has changed, except that I love you more now than I did then. Nothing has changed, except that I am older and appreciate you even more than I did then. Nothing has changed, except that you are part of who I am, and I am not complete without you. Nothing has changed, except that I define "love" by naming you. So once again I say 'Yes, I choose you as my partner for life.'"

(Repeat with second member of the married couple.)

6.

In the name of God and in the presence of these our friends and family, I, (NAME), once again take you, (NAME), to be my beloved partner in life. Time has not dimmed my devotion to you, and life has made us grow closer. Today, as always, we are united in the eyes of the One who called us to be a family. Thanks be to God for you. Amen.

(Repeat with second member of the married couple.)

7.

Officiant to first person: Repeat after me:

"I, (NAME), take you, (NAME), to be my wedded (husband, wife, partner, spouse) for as long as we both shall live. These words, spoken (number of years) years ago, are among the best words that I have ever spoken. I take you to be my best friend, my confidant, my love, for as long as we both shall live. I take you to be my companion, my partner, my inspiration, for as long as we both shall live. I take you to be my joy, my support, my focus, for as long as we both shall live. In sickness and in health, I offer myself to you and take you as my (husband, wife, partner, spouse). As we grow older together, I offer myself to care for you, to honor your wishes, and to love you."

(Repeat with second member of the married couple.)

8. (For a couple that has known brokenness, separation, or divorce and are reuniting)

(NAME), our journey has not been an easy one. At times we have been unworthy of the beautiful love that we have been given for one another. But we have stayed at the table, done the hard work of reconciliation, and I am ready to recommit myself to you without reservation. I take you again as my (husband, wife, partner, spouse), and look only to the future and the happiness we will share. In the name of God. Amen.

(Repeat with second member of the married couple.)

9.

(NAME), I am happy to have this opportunity to tell you once again, in front of our family and friends, how much I love you and how thrilled I am to continue sharing our journey through life. You have been and continue to be my best friend. More than that, you are part of who I am. I am not complete without you. Our shared journey has made me a better person. You are the source of most of my happiness, peace, and comfort. My spirit is lifted when I see you. Therefore, I am delighted to say with enthusiasm, "Yes, I choose you as the person with whom I wish to spend the rest of my life." Thank you for sharing your life and your love with me.

(Repeat with second member of the married couple.)

10. (For a couple with children)

(NAME), I give myself to you once again, and I thank you for the blessings of married life. I thank you for your love, for our beautiful children, (NAMES), and for the gift of tomorrow. I am yours; you are mine; and together we are family. Thanks be to God.

(Repeat with second member of the married couple.)

11.

Officiant: Repeat after me:

"(NAME), today I celebrate one of the best days of my life. It is the day that I said that I wanted to spend the rest of my life loving you and being loved by you. I celebrate the moment we first met, the time we first felt drawn to one another, the development of a love that has withstood differences of opinion, and the love that has enabled us to hold one another up when we needed each other. Today I celebrate the presence and activity of God as I have seen God in you again and again. It is with gratitude and joy that I renew my pledge to share the journey with you, and only you, as long as we both shall live."

(Repeat with second member of the married couple.)

SERVICES OF COMMITMENT

As mentioned in our introductory comments, many couples are choosing to avoid legal marriages. With that in mind, we offer two possible services to be helpful. We encourage you to re-read the introductory comments and "caveat" in the "For Your Consideration" section. The following orders of service should be considered suggestions, with the hope that you will move in creative ways to build an event which celebrates your relationship and moves you into a more committed partnership.

A Service of Commitment

Gathering Music

Gathering Words

Officiant: We come together to witness the commitment of two friends as they celebrate a relationship that has developed over time and has led them to want to share their love for each other with friends and family. (NAME and NAME) have invited us to be part of their lives. Let us pray:

Loving God, we gather in Your holy name as we witness and celebrate the love which (NAME and NAME) declare before us. We know that You are the essence of love. Your creation declares Your love for all humanity. You have created us to be together, to share ourselves with others, and to thrive when we know that we are loved. May the words spoken here today be meaningful to each of us as we seek to love one another. Amen.

(NAME and NAME), as we stand in the presence of these friends, family members, and witnesses, are you prepared to declare your love for each other and to make a commitment before them and before almighty God, that you love one another and intend to spend all of the remaining days of your life in faithfulness to one another? If so, answer "I do!"

Couple: I Do!

Officiant: Then in the presence of God and these witnesses, I ask you to declare your love and commitment to one another.

First Partner:

I, (NAME), stand before our family and friends, and in

the presence of Almighty God, and pledge to take you, (NAME), as my life partner, my best friend, and my love, for the rest of my days. I pledge to love, honor, and cherish you until death do us part.

Second Partner:

I, (NAME), stand before our family and friends, and in the presence of Almighty God, and pledge to take you, (NAME), as my life partner, my best friend, and my love, for the rest of my days. I pledge to love, honor, and cherish you until death do us part.

Officiant: Do you wish to exchange rings or some other symbol of your commitment to one another?

Couple: We do!

Officiant: (NAME), as you place the ring (or other symbolic object) on (NAME), please repeat these words after me:

(You may use your own words if preferred)

"In the presence of Almighty God and these witnesses, I place this ring upon your finger as a symbol of my love for you and my commitment to you. May it declare to all the world that you are mine and I am yours, so help me God."

Officiant: (NAME), as you place the ring (or other symbolic object) on (NAME), please repeat these words after me:

(You may use your own words if preferred) "In the presence of Almighty God and these witnesses, I place this ring upon your finger as a symbol of my love for you and my commitment to you. May it declare to all the world that you are mine and I am yours, so help me God."

Officiant: Declaration of a committed union!

Friends, Family members, and other guests, I declare

before God and before each of you that (NAME and NAME) have shared words of love and commitment to each other and have exchanged symbols of their commitment to each other. Therefore, in the name of our God, I declare before you that they are a committed couple, known from this day forward as partners in the journey of life. May God bless them and cause their love to grow in the years to come.

Let us pray: God of love and grace, we offer our prayers of gratitude that you have brought (NAME and NAME) together, enabled them to find love in one another, and allowed us to witness their expression of that love. May their love for each other be an example of your love for us, to all who observe it. Help them to demonstrate lives of love for one another and for all humanity, we ask in the name of Jesus, the Christ! Amen!

Congregation: The Lord's Prayer (in unison)

Our Father, who art in heaven, hallowed be thy name. Thy kingdom come, thy will be done, on earth as it is in heaven. Give us this day our daily bread, and forgive us our trespasses (*"debts" may be used*) as we forgive those (*"our debtors" may be used*) who trespass against us. And lead us not into temptation, but deliver us from evil, for thine is the kingdom, and the power, and the glory, forever. Amen.

Officiant: We have witnessed an act of love and we have heard words that declare trust and faithfulness between these two friends. We complete our act of worship and celebration by going to a reception where the party will continue. I send you out reminding you that life is all about love. Leave this place loving one another. Be kind to those who need kindness. Be gentle to those who need gentleness. Be generous to those who are in need. Be instruments of love, and thus instruments of God. Go in peace, and the peace of God go with you. Amen.

A kiss may be shared.

Music to depart

A non-religious ceremony of commitment

Gathering Music

Gathering Words
Officiant: Family and friends, today is a special day, a day rooted in a friendship that has blossomed into love. It is our privilege to have witnessed the flowering of this relationship. And now, we support (NAME and NAME), who wish to commit their lives to one another. We stand with them at this special moment as our affirmation that they will never stand alone. Just as they have one another, they also have us at their side.

A Poem or song that has special meaning may be shared.

Words of commitment
First partner: (NAME), today I acknowledge you as my companion on the journey of life. We have been through a great deal together, met many challenges, and supported and comforted one another. And now in the presence of our friends and family, I offer you an enduring place at my side, and ask the same from you. Life can be lonely, the world is a big place, and the nights are dark. But now, I welcome you as my partner, my anchor, and my light. May the promises made here today endure for as long as we both shall live.

[Repeated by the other partner.]
Officiant: Today we hear these words, and we offer our support to these two special people who come to us in the name of Love. May their shared journey be an inspiration to us all, and may our community be enriched by their

dedication to one another.

A Poem or song that has special meaning may be shared.

A Kiss of celebration may be shared.

Sending forth:

Go out into the world with an open heart and a thankful mind because these two beautiful people number us among their family and friends. We are grateful for the pathways of life that have brought them together, and now we walk with them, committed to making the world a better place.

Music to Depart

Acknowledgements

No significant work or accomplishment is ever achieved without assistance from countless people behind the person or persons whose names are attached to the project. With that in mind, we could begin our words of gratitude by thanking our great grandparents and so forth. But we will not. Instead, we will name a few of the folks who actually helped make this project become a reality.

First, our wives: Nancy and Lynn. These two amazing and wonderful women have offered their support and encouragement as we have used what might have been "family time" to create various prayers, vows, questions, etc. Their encouragement and suggestions have made this a better book. We owe them our gratitude as they have lightened our load during the periods when we have worked together and apart to find the right words for the book.

Second, The Reverend Barbara Sagat-Stover, ordained clergy of the Metropolitan Community Church. Barbara has helped us expand our understanding and broaden our inclusiveness as we have worked on this collection of wedding choices. She has guided us in our choice of words and made us more sensitive to the concerns of the LGBTQ community. Thank you, Barbara; you have made this a better book!

A third reader, Ann Norsworthy, retired Physician's Assistant, has also read the manuscript and added a lay person's perspective, as well as the value of a third reader. Her thoughtful and insightful suggestions were very helpful in making this a better tool for couples wanting to create meaningful weddings. We are very grateful for Ann's input and affirmation.

Finally, thanks to a friend, retired State Senator, and attorney Roger Katz for his legal consultation and guidance regarding the "Services of Commitment" section.

Once again, as was true for *Words for Your Wedding,* we are indebted to the Episcopal Church for the ability to use the traditional wedding service as it is found in the *Book of Common Prayer.* The freedom to use this material is a gift that reaches far beyond this book. It is a gift to all who will receive it.

About Atmosphere Press

Atmosphere Press is an independent, full-service publisher for excellent books in all genres and for all audiences. Learn more about what we do at atmospherepress.com.

We invite you to check out some of Atmosphere's latest releases, which are available at Amazon.com and via order from your local bookstore:

My Way Forward: Turning Tragedy into Triumph, by Molei Wright

In Pursuit of Calm, by Daniel Fuselier, PsyD

UFOs of the Kickapoo, by John Sime

Livin' on the Edge: A Guide to Your Abundance Seeds, by Tinker McAdams

There Are Some Secrets, by Sara Sass

Running Away From the Circus: Confessions of a Carnie Kid (Who Tried to become a Priest), by Nove Meyers

Mama: True Stories of Maternal Health in Malawi, by Caitlin Arlene

Out and Back: Essays on a Family in Motion, by Elizabeth Templeman

About the Authors

The Reverend Doctor David Glusker is a retired United Methodist clergy who served as the pastor of local churches in Maine and Massachusetts for twenty-six years, and as an ecumenical media minister, reaching people in northern New England, Canada, and part of the Mid-West for fourteen years. He is a graduate of Eastern Nazarene College (BA), Boston University School of Theology (M Div), and New York Theological Seminary (STM and D Min). He is married and has three surviving children, three step-children, and fourteen grandchildren. He and his wife, Nancy, live in Maine and worship at the Pleasant Street United Methodist Church in Waterville,

Maine, where the Reverend Dr. Thom Blackstone has served as the pastor.

Rev. Glusker is a past president of the Maine Council of Churches. He served as a short-term volunteer missionary in Jamaica, worked with his wife as a volunteer for hurricane relief in Texas for several years, has been a short-term volunteer pastor in Eleuthera, Bahamas, and served for ten years as a mission team leader for groups going to "Salud y Paz" in Panajachel, Guatemala. His carpentry abilities have enabled him to build simple furniture for school children, as well as a communion table for a local church, and has designed and built a medical clinic. At age eighty-three, he continues to look for ways to serve God and God's people.

In 1983, Rev. Glusker invited his good friend, the Rev. Dr. Peter Misner, to join him in creating a book that would help couples play a larger role in creating their own wedding ceremonies. *Words for Your Wedding* was published and proved to be a helpful tool for thousands of couples and officiants planning weddings. In 2019, he invited his pastor and friend, the Rev. Dr. Thom Blackstone, to join him in a similar project that would address the ever-changing and more inclusive world of the 21st century. Their goal is to help the human family be more loving and inclusive, to encourage acceptance of differences, and to serve the God of Love during their remaining years.

The Rev. Dr. Thom Blackstone is an active United Methodist clergy who has served United Methodist Churches in Maine and Rhode Island since 1991. He also served as adjunct professor of New Testament and Preaching at Bangor Theological Seminary in Maine and teaches preaching classes at the New England Local Pastors Licensing School and the denominational "Course of Study" Program administered by Wesley Theological Seminary in Washington, D.C. He is a graduate of Albright College (BA), Princeton Theological Seminary (M.Div.), and Emory University (Ph.D.). He completed his dissertation on the Book of Hebrews as an act of preaching under Dr. Fred Craddock in 1995. He is married to his wife, Lynn, and they have three adult children. He is also an avid amateur photographer, seeking to reflect spiritual transcendence by freezing moments of time.

Having served churches in some of Maine's most beautiful coastal towns, Rev. Blackstone has officiated at hundreds of weddings for parishioners and strangers alike, often making use of the first edition of *Words for Your Wedding*. He is honored to have the opportunity to update our language about marriage, while at the same time affirming the premise of the first edition: that the words we speak at weddings are powerful and important, and that those speaking those words should be empowered to choose words that express who they are and what they are promising to one another on their special day.